The
Best
Best Man

by Jacqueline Eames

London

W. Foulsham & Co. Ltd.

NEW YORK TORONTO CAPE TOWN SYDNEY

W. FOULSHAM & CO LTD
Yeovil Road, Slough, Berks., England

ISBN 0-572-00889-9

© W. FOULSHAM & CO LTD 1974

Printed in Great Britain by
St Edmundsbury Press, Bury St Edmunds, Suffolk

Contents

Foreword

A POPULAR MISCONCEPTION about the best man is that he is chosen for his role at the wedding on account of his colourful wit and glowing qualities. Nearer the truth of the matter is the fact that a best man is a human being. He often has little idea about wedding organization and probably bites his nails at the prospect of making a speech. He accepts the responsibilities of the post, because the groom, perhaps a lifelong friend, has asked this favour of him and he could not refuse.

This book presents the best man with a guide to all the technical details of a wedding from transport to fashion. He will see all the likely points of mishap and learn how to avoid them. He will realize that the most daunting prospect facing the best man – the wedding speech – can easily be overcome even without the talent and wit of a natural comedian.

1
Before the Day

Chapter 1

The Appointment

'To QUALIFY for the post the successful applicant will be sober, level headed, punctual, thorough, of harmonious disposition, tactful, witty and decisive.'

If you can fulfil all these qualifications your friend the groom will be lucky indeed to have such a model of perfection as his mentor.

These are the ideal qualities for the best men, but in reality it is rare to find them all in one person. To be honest, most best men are selected on the strength of a lifelong friendship and usually for no other reason. Successful best-man-ship is attained by the assimilation of facts about the wedding day and the ability to act as liaison officer between a large number of people and the source of information – the bride herself.

Basically the best man has seven major duties to perform:

1 Helping the groom to choose the ushers and to explain their duties for the wedding day;

2 Helping the groom to organize the stag party

and to see that he arrives home afterwards
without mishap;

3 Helping the groom to dress on the morning of
the wedding and getting him to church on time;
4 Handing the ring over to the groom at the
appropriate moment in the ceremony;
5 Organizing transport for the guests from the
church to the reception;
6 Making a speech at the wedding reception;
7 Seeing that the couple leave the reception on
time.

On paper it all sounds easy, but to do the job
properly, to be in command of the situation, to
see that everything runs smoothly, you will have
to know every detail of the wedding arrangements,
backwards, forwards, and sideways. There are
rarely disasters at a wedding, but if there are
snags – all eyes turn to the best man to solve the
problem. Be sure you know all the likely points of
mishap, well before the wedding day.

Sobriety

Maintaining a clear head amid the euphoria of the
wedding celebrations is vital for the best man. You
should be sober enough to see the groom to his
front door after the stag party. You should remain
sober on the wedding eve, so that the next day is
not spent fighting a hangover and you must remain
sober enough at the wedding reception to deliver
an articulate speech and to see the couple off the
premises at the right time.

Commonsense

One wonders how often, if ever, that joke situation
of the wedding ring falling down a grating in the
church has happened. It could happen of course
and if you want to take all adequate precautions –

buy a substitute gold band from Woolworths just
in case. No one can be absolutely sure how they are
going to react in an emergency, but if you are
prepared for the more obvious mishaps, such as
making a list of taxi firms in your area, in case the
car breaks down on the way to church – your
nerves will be in better shape on the wedding day.

Punctuality

It should go without saying that this is a vital
quality for the best man. If the wedding is to be
held early in the day and you know that almost
nothing short of a time bomb will get you out of
bed, then arrange for a telephone alarm call and
once you are up, stay up. If you do not have a
telephone, ask an understanding neighbour to
bang on the door until you answer. At a Register
Office wedding good time keeping is essential since
there is usually a string of weddings throughout the
day at about twenty-minute intervals. If one couple
is late, they may have to miss their turn altogether.

Thoroughness

Although the responsibilities of organizing a
wedding fall largely on the bride's family, you
must inform yourself about all the details, even
though many of them may not seem to be any
direct concern of yours. It is often suggested that
the groom should liaise closely with the chief
bridesmaid, but there could be a snag here. For
example, there may not be a bridesmaid; or she
may live at John O'Groats, when the wedding is
to be held at Land's End; or the eldest attendant
may be no more than six. The one person who
knows everything there is to know about the
wedding is the bride herself.

The Harmonious Disposition

The best man has to communicate with people of all ages and stations at the wedding, from the smallest bridesmaid to the oldest grandmother. It is part of your job to be charming to everyone. This could include appearing to be enthralled by the never-ending reminiscences about the bride's childhood from a doting aunt and then switching your attention to the page boy's chocolate-covered fingers before he makes a grab at the bride's veil. It goes without saying that you must look as though you are enjoying every minute.

Tact

You will be expected to see that the reception runs smoothly. Keep an eye open for dry corners and let the waiters know about people who seem to be overlooked. You might have to disengage the bride and groom from people who seem to be monopolizing their company – there is always one notorious bore at every wedding. If the vicar has decreed that no confetti should be thrown in the church grounds, make sure that you stop people from doing this. Check to see whether the vicar will allow photographs to be taken in church – if he will not, detail the ushers to warn people with cameras as they enter the church.

The Art Of Being Witty

Very few people have this accomplishment, and if you as the best man do not, then forget about trying to learn how to be the world's greatest wit before the wedding day – it simply will not work. Just concentrate on being sincere in your wedding speech and remember that most people are too busy talking and eating to be over-critical about what you say unless you waffle on for too long.

Chapter 2

Sundry Meetings and Discussions

YOUR ROLE as the best man begins from the moment you have been selected by the prospective groom and have agreed to undertake the responsibility.

As far as the bride's family is concerned preparations for the wedding will begin as soon as the engagement is announced formally, either in the newspaper, by means of a celebratory party, or simply by word of mouth. Three months is generally the accepted length of time to allow for detailed planning, although these days some churches and reception premises have to be booked months in advance, particularly for a Saturday wedding.

Unbreakable Rules
Make sure you know some of the rules and regulations laid down by the church authorities, although these will be explained to the bride and groom when they go to book the wedding.

Each church has its own parish boundaries and

if the bride and groom live in the parish where they are to be married the banns will be called from that church and there will be no further complications.

If one of the couple lives outside the parish boundaries the banns will have to be called from the two churches involved. If both live outside the parish where they are to be married then banns must be called at their own churches and the church where they are to be married. In addition one of the couple must guarantee to do one of two things. To take up residence within the parish where they are to be married for the fifteen days before the wedding, or to be put on the electoral roll of the church and attend the services there for six months before the wedding. When banns are called from churches other than the one where the couple are to be married, a certificate must be signed by the minister. This certificate should be handed to the minister performing the marriage ceremony on or before the wedding day.

If these circumstances should apply to the groom the banns certificate will be one of the documents you should have with you when you leave for the church on the morning of the wedding.

Priority Talks

If there are to be attendants at the wedding who include an adult bridesmaid, ask the groom to arrange a meeting for himself, the bride, the bridesmaid and yourself, so that you can discuss exactly what everyone will have to do before the wedding day. If, as we have already discussed, there are no bridesmaids – go ahead with the meeting anyway and get all the details from the bride herself.

At this stage you will need to know the following facts:

1   Where the wedding is to take place, the date
    and the time;
2   Where the reception is to take place;
3   How many people are to be invited;
4   What sort of reception it will be: a wedding
    breakfast, buffet or dance.

If the bride and groom both live locally it is likely that you will know the church and reception premises quite well, but nevertheless you could take a drive from the groom's home to the church and then on to the hotel to see exactly how long it takes and, most important, to find out what car parking facilities there are at both the church and reception grounds.

The number of guests is an important factor because it will determine the number of ushers required on the day, and the type of reception will determine some of the finer points of your duties.

The Invitations

Ideally these should go out from the bride's home six weeks before the wedding. The bride and groom could ask you to cast an eye over the guest list to see if there are any vital ommissions. It sometimes happens when you are dealing with a large number of people that close friends are left off by mistake while your mind is concentrating on all the distant relatives who must be invited. A fresh eye on the subject will often put matters right before any feelings are hurt.

In normal circumstances the invitation wording for a Church of England wedding will read:

Mr and Mrs Charles Hammond

request the pleasure of your company

at the marriage of their daughter

Jane Emily

to

Mr John Ian Mitchell

at 3 pm

on Saturday March 17th

at All Saints Church, Lands Lane, Harrow,

and afterwards at

The White Swan Hotel, Beech Grove, Harrow.

R.S.V.P.

45, Clement Avenue

Harrow

Middlesex

If the bride's father is dead, or her parents were divorced and her mother has remarried, the wording of the invitation could read:

Mr and Mrs Charles Smith

request the pleasure of your company

at the marriage of *her* daughter

Jane Emily

etc.

The confusing part of wedding invitation etiquette is that the bride's surname is not usually included on the wedding invitation, even if it should differ from that of her mother. If such a situation does exist, make sure that you at least have everyone's correct name and be prepared to tell people should they ask, particularly in connection with wedding presents to be sent to the bride's home before the wedding day.

The Ushers
Selection of the ushers should be made by the
groom with helpful hints thrown in by the best
man about the suitability of the choice. These are
usually from the groom's immediate circle of
friends, although a brother of the bride may find
himself doing the honours.

People tend to regard the ushers as also-rans,
but they should be kept aware of all the arrangements and details, so that one of them could take
over from you at a moment's notice, should the
need arise.

Ushers should be responsible, level-headed
people, but if their responsibilities extend to a
pregnant wife with two small children, or a lengthy
journey from one end of the country to the other
to attend the wedding, it might be better to make
another choice.

For a wedding of about a hundred people there
should be four ushers.

1 One will give out service sheets at the church
   door;
2 One will stand at the foot of the aisle to ask on
   which side of the church the guests wish to sit
   (bride's family and friends on the left; groom's
   on the right);
3 Another will stand half way down the aisle
   to usher people to their seats;
4 The fourth will be posted at the church door
   to escort the bride's mother to her seat on
   arrival at the church.

If the wedding is to be a very large affair you
should appoint a fifth usher to direct people to
car parks.

After the wedding ceremony the ushers should
help to organize transport for the guests from the

church to the reception and keep an eye on the food and drinks situation at the reception itself to see that there are no dry corners.

Punctuality is as vital for the ushers as it is for the best man for there is nothing worse than a late arrival panting down the aisle seconds before the bridal procession is due to start. It looks bad, it is bad and, worst of all, it upsets everyone else's careful planning. If one of the groomsmen is notoriously late for everything do find someone else.

Transport

Find out how many official cars are ordered for the wedding day. Depending on the number of attendants there are usually two for the journey from the bride's home to the church and three from the church to the reception.

Before the wedding:

1 One car is needed for the bride's mother and the attendants;
2 One car is needed for the bride and her father.

After the wedding:

1 One car for the bride and groom;
2 One car for the attendants;
3 One car for the bride's parents (unless they can arrange to leave their car at the church premises before the wedding begins).

The groom's parents are usually expected to provide their own transport.

Study the guest list with the bride and groom and tick off all the people who have transport for the wedding and then make a list of all the people who will need a lift. Try to fit everyone in somewhere.

Arriving at the wedding should be the responsibility of each guest who has replied to the invitation, but, if the church is a great distance away from the nearest main line station, some people would no doubt welcome a lift to the church. Try to find out exactly who this applies to and detail a few reliable friends to do a shuttle service from the station to the church. This is a better plan than relying on taxi firms, who are usually very busy on a Saturday, the most popular day for weddings.

Your Transport

Since the advent of the package-deal holiday honeymoons abroad have become the rule rather the exception, but Saturday departures are usually reserved for scheduled flights so it is extremely unlikely that a package-deal honeymoon will start immediately after the wedding reception. The first night is often spent at the new home or at a hotel until the flight is ready to leave. It is likely that the couple will use their own car, if they have one, to leave the reception. If this is the case the groom's car should be driven to the reception premises on the morning of the wedding and then your car should be used to drive the groom to the church.

If one can ever make a generalization about the qualifications of the best man the ability to drive must rank high on the list. While this is not an essential from a personality point of view, a best man with his own set of wheels can be a godsend in an emergency. It is a wise precaution to make sure that if the best man does not drive one of the ushers can.

The Wedding Present List

There is no obvious reason why the best man

should expect to find himself involved with the
bride's wedding present list, but it is surprising how
many find themselves dealing with this unexpected
hazard.

In the first place there is the confidential guest
who will take the best man to one side and say
'I'd like to buy them something rather special, but
I'd like it to be a surprise – perhaps you'd know
what they would like?' If the generous donor has
seen and mentally rejected everything on the
wedding list, it will be up to you to use your tact
and diplomacy to find out what that 'special
something' could be without giving the game away
and, hopefully, without landing the couple with a
hideous white elephant.

Generally speaking the question of presents is
dealt with in one of two ways. The first way is to
deposit a wedding list with a department store
which offers this rather specialized service to the
bride. It is usually known as 'The Wedding List
Department', 'The Bride's Book' or 'The Wedding
Gift Bureau'. The bride will visit the store and,
together with an assistant from the bureau, make
a list of all the items she would like to see in her
new home. These consist of reasonably priced gifts
of china, glass, cutlery, linens and home accessories.
The representative from the bureau will then make
a comprehensive list of the items, their design,
colour and quantity, which is then held by the store
as a master copy. The bride takes a second copy
and retains it for her own use. When people start
to ask what the couple would like, the bride can
tell the donor which store has her list. The donor
can ring or visit the store ask to see the list, make
a choice and pay the bill. The item is at once
deleted from the master copy, the gift dispatched

to the bride and duplication of presents is, with luck, avoided.

The alternative method of dealing with the list is slightly more hazardous. The bride makes her own wedding list and sends it around to her friends as they ask for it. The donor will choose the gift he or she intends to buy and will cross it off the list, returning the list to the bride, ready to send on to the next person. As you can imagine one master list will take a long time to circulate around all the guests, and the last people to receive it will find themselves left with the most expensive or least interesting items. It can help to speed up the process if you keep a copy of the list so that, if people should ask you as the best man what the bride would like, you can read the list to them and ask them to make a couple of choices. Ring the bride and ask if the items selected have already been bought and if not, you can then relay her preference to the donor. Some duplication of presents is inevitable, because there are always people who will buy without bothering to check. The thought is often 'Oh glasses will be OK – you can never have too many glasses'. This is probably quite true for such useful objects, but problems occur when the couple find themselves faced with the disposal of two dozen step-ladders.

Reception Rehearsal

Before the wedding day draws too close, you should try to visit the reception premises with the bride and groom. The bride is bound to want to see the banqueting manager to discuss the flower arrangements, the cake, the menu and the number of guests invited to the wedding. Take the opportunity to hear what is being said and so furnish yourself with more facts. You can then ask the manager about the general procedure for receptions at this particular hotel. He may tell you that you must vacate the premises by 6.30 pm because they are expecting a hundred people in afterwards for a Rotary dinner. A member of his staff may act as toastmaster for the occasion and it will make your life easier on the day of the wedding if you can meet the toastmaster before the occasion and discuss the sequence of speeches and work out a rough timetable. You will probably have to refresh his memory on the wedding day but at least the facts will be in your own mind. Take a look at the likely changing rooms which will be given to the bride and groom for the afternoon and see what the car parking facilities are like.

If the hotel cannot provide a toastmaster for the occasion then the wedding guests and the speeches, with the exception of your own, will have to be announced by you. In any case, because it will be vital for you to know exactly what time you are all expected to leave the premises, you will be watching the clock.

Chapter 3

A Question of Fashion

WHAT TO WEAR at the wedding will be your next major point of discussion. You must get the bride's own views about this – don't rely on the groom for he may not agree with what she says and you may be needed to mediate. Happily most brides are so concerned about their own and their attendants' clothes that they will say no more than 'Oh a suit will be fine', or 'Morning suits for all the principal men.' These will include the groom, the ushers, both fathers and yourself.

Formal Dress
If the wedding is to be a very formal affair, the words 'morning dress' can appear on the wedding invitation under the R.S.V.P., but this is not general practice and the bride's wishes are usually spread by word of mouth.

Buying a morning suit is a very expensive business, but if you are going to use this opportunity then buy a suit at one of the better department stores. It won't be cheap, but it should last a lifetime. All the accessories: shirt, grey topper, grey gloves, can be bought as well. You can use a grey tie for a wedding, but never, never, a black one. Black shoes and socks are the best choice with a grey morning suit.

Accessories such as the hat and gloves can be a nuisance at the wedding because you can only wear them for the photographs. The rest of the time is spent carrying them – or leaving them in in the church porch to get mixed up with those belonging to someone else. But if you plan to lead a bright social life with trips to Ascot every year it is probably worth buying the accessories.

The Tailor Made Suit

If you do not know a good local tailor who can make you a morning suit, there are tailors who can offer the most superb styling providing you have a great deal of money to spend. Your own ideas can be expertly translated into an impeccable suit but you must expect to pay a great deal of money for it.

One designer of men's clothes once made a wise remark about the morning suit. He pointed out that unless the wearer is very tall and rather slim the long tails of the morning coat can throw the body out of all proportion. The frock coat – a nostalgic throwback to Edwardian times offers an enjoyable alternative for the shorter man. The coat comes down to the knee and it can be single or double breasted; the collar and lapels can be trimmed with velvet. It can look very sophisticated when it is worn with a pale silk stock swathed around the throat. Trousers can be pin-striped or in the same fabric as the coat.

Traditional morning suits are either all grey or

have black tailed coat and pin-striped trousers, sometimes worn with a cream waistcoat. There is no reason why you should not choose colour for your morning suit. Dark blue, lovat green, wine or brown are all quite acceptable providing that the wearer has the bearing and confidence to carry off the unusual.

The cravat is a very popular addition to modern morning dress and should always be worn with a high winged collar. The colour of the cravat is purely a matter of personal preference, but the following guide may give you some ideas about ways to tone the accessories to the basic colour of the suit.

Suit	Shirt	Waistcoat	Cravat/Tie/Stock	Shoes/Socks
Black	White	Grey/Cream Black	Grey/Cream	Black Black
Grey	Blue	Grey	Blue/Grey	Black Black
Brown	Cream	Cream/Brown	Cream/Brown	Brown Brown
Green	Cream	Cream/Green	Cream/Grey Green	Black Black
Wine	Cream	Wine/Cream	Old Rose	Black Black
Blue	Pale Blue	Blue/Grey	Dark Blue	Black Black

Colour in morning dress is fun – for the rich anyway, but if you are considering buying an expensive suit specially made it is probably better to opt for traditional colours. The current relaxation of many established rules of etiquette and the trend of finding one's own style may not last as long as your morning suit, bought in a mood of colourful and sophisticated abandon.

Hiring a Morning Suit

A remark one often hears at a wedding is that a man could buy a morning suit twice over with the money he has spent on a lifetime of hiring fees. Nevertheless this can only apply to someone who spends a great deal of his time at very formal weddings and other social occasions. For the majority a lounge suit is often appropriate enough.

MOSS BROS. COVENT GARDEN, LONDON, WC2 have been well established for years in the hire business in England, and their name is known the world over. They can supply both the traditional black coat and pin stripes or the plain grey morning suit. One of their most surprising accessories is a pair of spats, perhaps for those who might consider the frock coat!

It would be senseless to try to enumerate all the fourty-four Moss Bros shops and six thousand agents in Britain and Europe, but you could contact the main shop at Covent Garden and find out your nearest branch if you do not already know it.

You should bear in mind that the summer months are very popular for weddings and for a number of other social functions such as Ascot. It is wise to reserve your wedding suit well in advance of the wedding date and of course you must get it back within the time specified otherwise you will find yourself paying a surcharge.

Occasionally you will find that the bride has very strong views about what the men should wear. She may have a particular colour scheme in mind for herself, her attendants and the church flowers. For example, her own dress may be white with a pink sash, her bridesmaids and page boys may be dressed in sweet pea colours of blue, pink and lilac to echo the flowers in her bouquet, church decorations and reception flowers. It could work well if the groom, best man and ushers wore lilac silk cravats with pale grey morning suits.

There are no hard and fast rules about who should pay for what at the wedding, and nowadays the generally accepted procedure is that attendants pay for their own clothes. Strictly speaking this should not apply to additional items in the mens' dress so, if you do come up against a problem like this, you could tactfully point out to the groom that he or the bride should pay for silk cravats to be made.

The Wedding Suit

As any women will tell you, a wedding is always a good excuse for a new outfit and there is no reason why this should not also apply to men too. Since velvet suits have made such an impact on the fashion scene more and more men are adopting this fabric, in 'old master' colours for their weddings, and sources of supply for these are now on the increase. Velvet and lace will combine well for a special occasion like a wedding. Silk shirts with a lace jabot and cuffs can make an opulent impact on the wedding audience. As best man, however, take care that you do not outshine the groom. Cream silk shirts and ties are another good choice with most dark-toned velvets. A simply cut two- or three-piece lounge suit is perhaps the best buy of all because it automatically becomes part of your everyday wardrobe after the great event. It is well worth looking around some of the big departmental stores for off-the-peg styles imported from Scandinavia, Italy and Yugoslavia. Lightweight suits, well cut and in conservative colours, are a good buy for those who are stock sizes and will cost far less than a tailor-made. You can dress up a simple style with printed silk or cotton shirts with matching ties. A dizzy striped or spotted bow tie can be fun to wear for a wedding – particularly if it has the added bonus of a St Laurent label! Don't automatically opt for the traditional look, after all a wedding is cause for celebration.

Whatever you wear one rule is always the same: shoes must be polished to a mirror-shine (and you should remind the groom to remove the price tag from new shoes!).

Clothes at the Civil Wedding

There are no rules about the right and wrong clothes to wear at the register office. Most Registrars will see blue jeans and tee-shirts, blazers, sport's jackets, lounge suits and even morning suits all pass before their bewildered eyes during the course of one-day's work.

Your choice of clothes will depend on the views of the bride and groom. Take your cue from them, imitate their style but do not outshine them.

One point which many people forget is that the traditional white wedding dress with full train and veil were designed to create an impact inside the church where the aisle can show the garment off to its full advantage. Very formal attire like this is not really suitable for the often cramped conditions at most Register Offices and you will find that, in the same way, a morning suit will dominate rather than complement the surroundings.

The Buttonholes

The white carnation used to be the traditional buttonhole for weddings and still is popular. However, so much can be done nowadays to change the colour of flowers by dipping and tinting that it is possible for the groomsmen to be more adventurous in their choice. The carnation is one flower which dyes extremely well to fit in with a particular colour scheme, but the florist must be given plenty of warning.

Convention holds that the groom should pay for his own buttonhole and for those of the best man and the ushers. These should be ordered at least three weeks before the wedding from a local florist and collected before the ceremony. If the wedding is to take place on unfamiliar ground the bride could order the buttonholes together with all the other wedding flowers and arrange for them to be delivered to the reception premises. The best man and groom can collect them when they leave the groom's going-away clothes, before going on to the church. Possible alternatives to the white carnation are the clove (red) carnation, the garnet rose, the cornflower, the orchid or the camellia although the latter is sometimes rather fragile.

Chapter 4

The Stag Party

TRADITIONALLY the stag party takes place on the eve of the wedding – but the X-certificate stories about the consequences of these last-minute celebrations are too numerous to be recounted here. Try if possible to persuade the groom to hold the party a few days before the event, to give everyone a good chance to recover from the predictable results of over-indulgence in sentimental alcohol.

The majority of stag parties are very informal, usually held in the local pub and followed by an inexpensive meal. Chinese and Indian restaurants seem to rank high as a final port of call for a bachelor night out, possibly because they are more willing to welcome late-night eaters than many others. The date, time and location of the party are spread by word of mouth and it would be kind if you were to offer to contact a number of those invited. The guests will normally include close friends of the groom, brothers of the bride and sometimes the groom's father, but, even if he is a determined adolescent, the generation gap can put a blight on the proceedings; and the presence of a woman at such a function certainly will. In any case the bride and her friends can have their own rival celebration and by all accounts these are very enjoyable.

It is wise to book a table if you are planning to eat at a restaurant after the pub outing, so that there are no last-minute disappointments and all the party can be seated together.

At one time the stag party was a very formal affair and the guests wore black tie and dinner jackets for the occasion, but this was in an era when men's drinking clubs were a good deal more popular than they are today.

Traditionally the groom should pay for the entire evening's entertainment, but nowadays drinks for an entire evening, plus the cost of a meal for twenty or so voracious men, could be astronomical. Unless the groom can afford it you should explain that the meal is optional and at guests' own expense.

It is a good idea to walk to the pub or restaurant, if they are in your vicinity, or at least take a taxi. Nothing could be more unfortunate than being stopped by the police for driving under the influence of euphoric alcohol a few days before the wedding. Whatever you decide, do not allow the groom to drive.

On the stag night you should collect the groom from his home and escort him to the pub and offer to take charge of the kitty. You should know what sort of drinks your friends like, spirits or beer, so make sure that the groom has enough cash. You could take along some spare cash of your own – the groom can always pay you back if funds run short.

It has been known for a best man to take his duties seriously enough to exist on half a pint of beer for the whole evening, but, providing you do not intend to drive, why not enjoy the occasion? Everyone else will.

The stag party is a good opportunity for you to test your speech-making powers. Everyone will have made some cracks about the groom's last bachelor minutes ebbing away and there is no reason why you should not add your own comments. You should add your congratulations too: assure the groom that he has done the right thing and wish him all the luck in the world; after an evening of ragging he'll probably think he needs it!

Your last duty of the night is to see the groom to his front door. Do not leave until you are quite sure he is inside.

Chapter 5

The Week Before
the Wedding

The Go-Between

The relay system established earlier in the wedding preparations between yourself and the bride, groom and ushers will now be vitally important: any snags at this stage could affect procedures on the wedding day. The best idea is to make 'A LIST OF THINGS TO DO' and tick each item off one by one, when each query has been dealt with to the satisfaction of everyone concerned. The following list should give you some idea of the points you should have in mind.

1   Has the groom bought the wedding ring?
2   Has everyone who needs one ordered his wedding suit:
    a) Groom?
    b) Ushers?
    c) Yourself?
    NB Make sure that none of the main participants is planning to leave the collection of a morning suit until the morning of the wedding.

3 *Flowers*
   a) If the groom is ordering buttonholes from a local florist, does the florist know where to deliver the goods (the groom's home)?
   b) If you are collecting the buttonholes on behalf of the groom, have you contacted the florist to check that the flowers will be ready when you call?
   c) If the bride is arranging all the flowers including the men's buttonholes, has she arranged to leave the flowers at the reception premises or in the church vestry?

4 *Transport*
   a) Have you made a list of taxi firms in your area, in case the car breaks down on the way to the church?
   b) If neither you or the groom will be using a car on the day of the wedding:
      i) Is a taxi ordered to take you and the groom to the church?
      ii) Do you have transport from the church to the reception?
      iii) Do all the guests have adequate transport?
   c) If the bride and groom do not have a car, or they are not planning to use one for their honeymoon:
      i) Have you ordered a car to take them to the station/air terminal/new home?

5 Are the groom's documents in order?
   a) Passport;
   b) Driving licence;
   c) Traveller's cheques/foreign currency if they are honeymooning abroad.
   d) Has he remembered all the necessary innoculations?

e) Has he remembered to collect the banns certificate from his local minister (if he lives outside the parish where he is to be married)?

f) Does he have all the necessary insurances, travel tickets etc. for travelling on the continent by car?

6 Do you know how much the wedding fees will cost? The groom is responsible for fees to the minister, organist, choir, bellringers. There may be additional tips to the verger, but generally the minister will charge one comprehensive price and pay the people concerned himself.

7 Do you have enough spare cash for the wedding day? – Remember banks are not open on a Saturday.

8 Does the groom have enough money for both the wedding day and his honeymoon?

9 Have you checked on the layout of the church. i.e. the location of the vestry?

10 Does the minister have strong views about:

a) the time you are expected to arrive at the ceremony – naturally you will be expected to be early, but sometimes the minister will ask to meet you and the groom in the vestry twenty minutes before the ceremony begins to pay the fees before rather than after the wedding.

b) Confetti: some ministers have very strict views about waste paper, particularly when it is blowing around in their church grounds – you can be sure that this will apply to confetti. Detail an usher to mention this as people enter the church.

c) Photographs: views vary about the possibilities of taking photographs inside the church. The official photographer may be permitted to take shots of the couple signing the register in the vestry and perhaps one as they walk back down the aisle after the ceremony. You can be sure that all ministers will object to a host of light bulbs popping throughout the ceremony. Ushers should warn people with cameras as they arrive at the church. Nothing could be more embarrassing than the vicar calling a halt to the proceedings to admonish amateur photographers.

11 Does the groom have all the necessary clothes for his honeymoon?

12 Have you collected service sheets from the bride's home?

13 Has the bride remembered that her going-away clothes must be left at the reception premises before the wedding, together with her honeymoon luggage?

14 Does the hotel staff know that you are coming to deposit the groom's luggage and going-away clothes before the wedding ceremony?

15 Have you spoken to the manager of the hotel about what time you are all expected to leave the premises?

16 Do the ushers know what each should be doing on the wedding day?

17 Is there anything you can do to help the bride's family such as:
a) Transporting the cake;
b) Collecting flowers for the church or reception;
c) Helping with the marquee (if reception is to be held in a garden)?

18 Is everyone agreed on the sequence of events at the reception (see Chapter Nine for details)?

19 Has the groom remembered to remove the price tag from the bottom of his shoes (if they are new)?

20 Have you remembered the bride and groom's wedding present?

21 Have you reminded the bride's family that any telegrams delivered to their home on the morning of the wedding must be brought along to the reception?

22 Is the groom's new house insured against theft? Nothing could be worse than all the wedding presents being stolen while the couple are away. As any policeman will tell you, newly married couples are a particularly vulnerable target for the lighter-fingered members of our community. Someone from the bride's family could perhaps check on the premises while the couple are away, otherwise a new neighbour could be asked to keep an eye open for intruders.

23 Do you have an umbrella, just in case?

24 Are you keeping the groom calm?

The Wedding Rehearsal

Sometimes a minister will specially request an informal rehearsal for all the principal people involved in the wedding ceremony. This is usually necessary only when the wedding is to be a very large, formal affair, with a large number of attendants, or if the bride and groom are of different religions.

The rehearsal is held inside the church a few days before the wedding or perhaps on the wedding eve. It is a splendid opportunity to be introduced to the vicar, to examine the size of the gratings in the church and to ask any questions which are bothering you.

Unusual Wedding Presents from the Best Man
Although you will probably be too busy to do it
yourself it is a grand idea to try to organize someone to take a cine camera along to the wedding.
Most ministers will forbid their use inside the
church, but there is no reason why a film cannot
be made of the reception and departure of the
couple. There is a tremendous difference between
the stiff formality of the official wedding groups
when the bride and groom are acutely aware of
their newly married status, and the more relaxed
gaiety of the reception. A well-edited film can be
a superb wedding present from the best man to the
bride and groom.

Another good idea which will require permission
from the minister is to have a special recording of
the ceremony, transferred to a twelve-inch LP, a
cassette or a tape.

Outwitting the Weather
In the temperate but highly erratic climate of
Britain the weather will often catch people unawares at a wedding. You at least can be prepared
for the worst by taking a couple of large black
umbrellas along to the wedding with you. Big
black ceremonial or carriage umbrellas can be
hired. If the weather looks uncompromisingly
fine, you can always leave them in the car.

2
The Day

Chapter 6

Getting to the Church on Time

WHEN IT actually comes to the day of the wedding you will probably need little advice on ways to make yourself wake up in good time. You will probably be up half the night anyway, practising your wedding speech in front of the mirror. Once you are up and about, ring the groom to see that he is not snoring away his last bachelor minutes.

Opinions are divided about the need to ring the bride's home to see if her parents need any help. On one hand you may be roped in for an unforeseen trip to collect four dozen sausage rolls forgotten by the caterer, on the other hand you want to be regarded as the world's best best man, so it is probably safer to check that everything is fine at their end and avoid last-minute panics later in the day.

The time that you actually arrive at the groom's house to escort him to the church will depend on the length of the journey, and you should by now have checked all this out. If you have offered to collect buttonholes on behalf of the groom do this before you arrive at his home. As you leave the house check the following:

1 Money;
2 Service sheets;
3 List of taxi firms.

If the wedding is to be held at a local church, arrive at the groom's home about an hour and a half before the service is due to begin.

Traditionally one of your duties is to help the groom to dress, but unless his nerves are really shot to pieces, he should be able to perform this function quite adequately. You will, however, need to check over all his documents – two minds on the subject are invariably better than one – but under conditions of stress, i.e. your speech and his nerves, it is better to make a written list.

Cases packed and his going-away clothes arranged over a hanger you will leave his house with the following:

1 Honeymoon case;
2 Going-away clothes;
3 Buttonholes;
4 Service sheets;
5 Documents: driving licence and insurance, traveller's cheques, foreign currency, travel tickets, banns certificate (if necessary), passport, innoculation certificates;
6 A list of taxi firms;
7 Money;
8 Telegrams;
9 Umbrellas;
10 WEDDING RING (plus pieces of gold and silver for a Catholic ceremony).

Your first port of call is the reception premises to deposit the groom's case, car and going-away clothes. Telegrams can be left with the receptionist.

If the reception is to be held a long distance from the church the groom's belongings should be left in your car carefully arranged over the seat. If the groom is to use his car for the honeymoon, arrange to leave it at the reception premises the day before the ceremony, otherwise someone else will have to drive it from the church to the reception.

You should arrive at the church about three-quarters of an hour before the ceremony is due to start. Time for a swift pint before the service? Well, why not? Although this practice will never be approved by members of the clergy or by the bride, experience shows that the groom and his staff will often meet in a local tavern to discuss final points of procedure over a last bachelor beer.

Buttonholes are secured and service sheets handed over to the appropriate usher. The best man and groom will go over to the church to see the vicar and pay the fees before the ceremony (unless arranged otherwise). There are usually a few minutes to spare while the official photographer takes the obligatory photograph of the groom and best man shaking hands in the church porch and then everyone takes their places for the arrival of the guests and finally the bride herself.

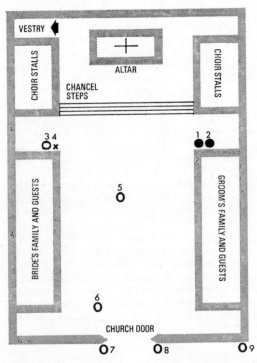

Fig. 1 *Church Seating*

1. Groom
2. Best Man
3. Bride's Mother
4. Seat for Bride's Father
5. and 6. Usher (Guests to their seats)
7. Usher (to give out hymn sheets)
8. Usher (Escort for Bride's Mother)
9. Usher (To direct Guests to Car Parks)

Chapter 7

The Ceremony

THE BRIDE'S mother should be one of the last people to arrive at the church. She usually travels to the church with the bridesmaids, who remain in the church porch to wait for the arrival of the bride. One of the ushers should escort the bride's mother to her seat in the front pew on the left of the chancel steps facing the altar. The bride's mother should leave room for her husband to take his place when he has given his daughter away to her new husband.

As soon as the bride arrives, the ushers should move quietly to their seats before the procession begins.

The full choral service in the Church of England takes about thirty minutes from start to finish. The minister will meet the bride in the church porch and the procession will begin with the chief chorister leading the way with the standard Cross. Behind him range the choir, the minister, the bride on her father's right arm and then the attendants in order of seniority.

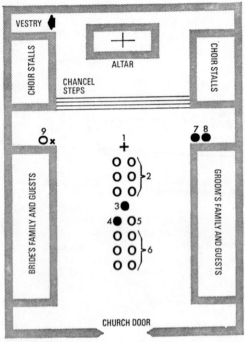

Fig. 2 *Procession*

1. Chief Chorister
2. Choir
3. Minister
4. Bride's Father
5. Bride
6. Attendants
7. Groom
8. Best Man
9. Bride's Mother
x. Space for Bride's Father

The organist will be watching to see that everyone is ready and when they are he will play the entrance music selected by the bride. This is usually a slow march or a reasonably gentle piece of music. The bride may choose to enter to the first hymn.

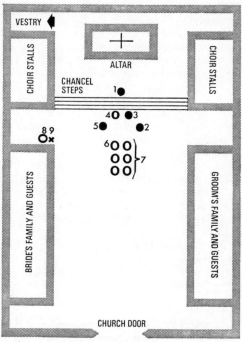

Fig. 3 *At the Chancel Steps*

1. Minister
2. Best Man
3. Groom
4. Bride
5. Bride's Father
6. Chief Bridesmaid
7. Attendants
8. Bride's Mother
9. Space for Bride's Father

As the first chords are played the congregation will rise to their feet and at this moment the best man and groom move from their seats to the chancel steps, standing a little to the right so that the choir and minister have room to walk through to the chancel.

When the choir has taken its place and the bridal party is assembled at the chancel steps the chief bridesmaid should step forward and take the bride's bouquet so that both her hands are free when the time comes to put on the ring.

Where there are no bridesmaids the bride can pass her bouquet to her father who can turn and hand it to the bride's mother, if the front pew is near enough to the chancel steps. In a large church the pews may be some feet away from the bridal party. In this case ask the minister before the service begins if a pew hassock could be strategically placed near the bridal party for the bouquet to rest on until the bride's father can hand it over to the bride's mother when his part in the ceremony is over.

If the aisle is very narrow, the bride's father and the best man should stand slightly behind the bridal couple, moving forward only when it is time for them to play their part in the ceremony.

The Order of Service

This will vary according to the wishes of the minister performing the ceremony, or those of the couple concerned. Some ministers often prefer to conduct the marriage before any hymns are sung and the address may be made from the altar or from the chancel steps.

Shown below is a typical order of service:

ENTRANCE MUSIC

HYMN

THE MARRIAGE

THE PSALM

PRAYERS (at the altar)

THE ADDRESS
HYMN
THE BLESSING
SIGNING OF THE REGISTER
(choir or organ music)
EXIT MUSIC

After the first hymn the minister will begin the marriage cermony with the words: 'Dearly beloved, we are gathered together here in the sight of God . . .'. The first words to the assembled company will explain the significance of marriage and the reasons why it was originally ordained. The minister calls on the congregation to declare any impediment to the marriage with the words: 'Therefore if any man can show just cause, why they may not lawfully be joined together, let him now speak, or else hereafter for ever hold his peace'. The minister will then ask the bride and groom if they know of any lawful impediment to their marriage, pointing out that if there is such an impediment, the marriage will not be valid.

'I require and charge you both . . .'

The minister then asks each of the couple in turn whether they are prepared to accept the other in marriage, according to the laws of the Church:

'Wilt thou have this woman to thy wedded wife?'
And to the bride:
'Wilt thou have this man to thy wedded husband?'
Both should answer 'I will'.
The minister will then ask:
'Who giveth this woman to be married to this man?'
The bride's father will say nothing, but he will

pass his daughter's right hand to the minister. The groom will take her hand with his right hand.

Repeating the words after the minister, the groom will make his vow first:

'I . . . , take thee . . . , to my wedded wife . . .'

They release their hands and the bride will take the groom's right hand in her own.

Repeating the words after the minister the bride will make her vow:

'I . . . , take thee . . . , to my wedded husband . . .'

When the vows have been completed the minister will offer the best man the open face of the prayer book, on which he should place the ring. The groom will take the ring and place it on the third finger of the bride's left hand with the words:

'With this ring, I thee wed . . .'

At this point in the ceremony the bride's father and the best man should return to their seats at the front of the church while the rest of the service continues. The minister will wait until they have taken their places before he asks the bride and groom to kneel and the rest of the congregation to pray. A blessing follows the prayers and then the minister will lead the bride and groom to the altar while the congregation sings the psalm.

The prayers that follow may be said or intoned, whichever the bride and groom prefer, or the minister will follow the usual custom of the church. The address usually follows the prayers, and the final hymn will conclude the service.

Signing the Register

The minister will then lead the bride and groom into the vestry. The congregation will sit and listen to the choir or the organist while the register is being signed. As soon as the bride and groom move into the vestry, the rest of the bridal party will follow. This will include both sets of parents, the attendants, who should all move off in a line, and yourself. Make sure that someone has remembered the bride's bouquet – if you should see it lying in the front pew, carry it through to the vestry yourself, as the bride will need it for her exit from the church.

In the vestry there is a round of congratulations, kisses and handshaking and then the bride and groom will sign the register. The bride signs first in her single name. When the couple have both signed, the minister will ask for two witnesses, who must be over the age of eighteen. The best man and the chief bridesmaid are usually requested to do this, but sometimes the minister will ask the fathers of the bride and groom to sign, because their names appear automatically on the marriage certificate and there will be no problems in deciphering the signatures should it ever be necessary.

One or two photographs may be taken while the register is being signed and then the bride and groom will lead the recession (that is, the pro-cession back down the aisle) from the church. The organist will strike up the exit music which is invariably a triumphal march and the bell ringers, hearing the notes of the organ, will chime forth the glad tiding to all and sundry.

Her bouquet restored to her, the bride walks on her husband's left side, leaving his sword arm free to defend her (this probably applied quite often in the olden days!). If the minister has asked that all the fees should be paid after the ceremony, the best man will stay behind in the vestry to settle the accounts, while the recession is in progress.

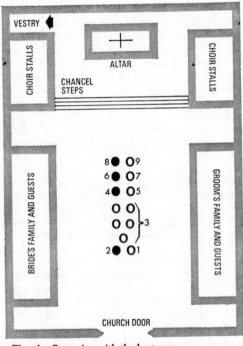

Fig. 4 *Recession with the best man*

1. Bride
2. Groom
3. Attendants
4. Groom's Father
5. Bride's Mother
6. Bride's Father
7. Groom's Mother
8. Best Man
9. Chief Bridesmaid

The Photographs

Official photographs usually take about twenty minutes to complete and you, as best man, will appear in several of these. Most couples will want at least one large group photograph of all the close

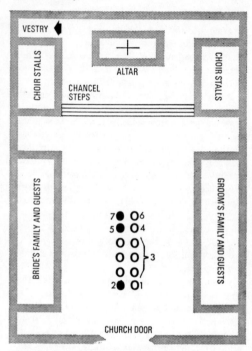

Fig. 5 *Recession without the best man*

1. Bride
2. Groom
3. Attendants (including Chief Bridesmaid)
4. Bride's Mother
5. Groom's Father
6. Groom's Mother
7. Bride's Father

relatives and it is the organization of just such a shot which will take the time. People are so busy shuffling from one foot to the other that either aunt Emily is completely hidden, or a man standing immediately behind the bride is giving the impression that it is not he but the bride who is wearing the top hat! Your voice of sanity can help the photographer to arrange all the small people in the front row and make sure that those behind are looking over the shoulders of the row in front and not over the top of their heads.

Rainy weddings are unfortunate and nearly always catch people unawares, but the excited bride and groom are less likely to notice the weather than the guests who may not be able to take refuge in the church porch because there is another wedding going on inside. They are forced to stand around with their straw hats collapsing around their faces and their silk suits clinging to their legs. In this case it is wise to cut out all the group photographs and take only one or two of the couple themselves. Most photographers automatically carry flashlights and will be equipped to take photographs on the reception premises if time and space permits.

When the ritual of photographs is over the bride and groom should be the first to leave for the reception and you should escort them to their car. The bridesmaids will leave next, followed by the bride's parents in their own car if it has been left at the church before the wedding. Transport for all the guests from the church to the reception should have been organized before the wedding day, so that there are no last-minute panics.

Seeing the guests off the church premises should be one of your duties, but you will be better employed at the reception, so slip away as soon as you can, leaving the ushers to cope in your absence. Ask one of them to check the church porch to see that there are no hats, gloves or service sheets lying around.

Chapter 8

Other Weddings and Circumstances

The Second Wedding in the Church of England
There has been a certain amount of relaxation in
the views of some ministers about remarrying a
divorced person in the established Church, but it is
still a very rare occurrence. Most ministers still
hold the very rigid belief that in the eyes of God
a marriage is valid to death and whatever the
circumstances, while both participants are still
alive, another marriage is not possible let alone
permissible.

Remarriage of widowed people is of course,
quite acceptable, but the minister must be consulted
for his views on a number of points. In the first
place he may feel that the bride should not wear a
veil, although he is unlikely these days to object to
her wearing white. He may feel that the choice of
certain hymns and music are not appropriate for a
second wedding; he may object to the pealing of
bells or the need for attendants.

In most cases, however, the ceremony and
organization will be exactly the same as for a first

wedding in church and the duties of the best man will also be the same.

The Service of Blessing

A blessing service is a brief, simple ceremony to bless the marriage of people who hold different religious beliefs, or in rare cases when one or other have been divorced. There are no hymns, bells or any of the conventional trappings. The bride and groom, together with a few friends, will meet in the church as for a normal service. The minister conducting the service will give a brief address, followed by prayers to bless the marriage and there is sometimes a gospel reading. There are no duties for the best man to perform at the ceremony, but if a reception follows the blessing, he will be required to help with the organization and possibly to make a speech.

The Double Wedding

Since most girls would be extremely reluctant to share the limelight on their wedding day it is usually only twins or sisters in the same age group, who share the same friends, who would welcome a double wedding.

The procedures are the same as for a wedding for one couple in that there will be a best man for each groom and attendants for the brides. Meetings and discussions will take place between six rather than three people (two brides, two grooms and two best men). One important point which must be established early on is what everyone should wear. If there are to be nearly a dozen people at the front of the church there should be a certain sense of uniformity in their dress – try to imagine how it will look from where the congregation is sitting.

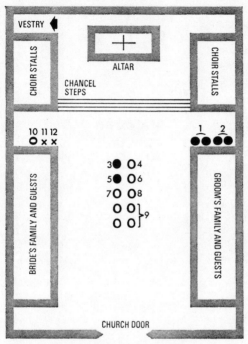

Fig. 6 *The Double Wedding procession*

1. Groom and Best Man (A)
2. Groom and Best Man (B)
3. Bride's Father
4. Bride (A)
5. Escort for Bride (B)
6. Bride (B)
7. Chief Bridesmaid (A)
8. Chief Bridesmaid (B)
9. Attendants
10. Mother of both Bride's
11. Seat for Bride's Father
12. Seat for Escort (B)

If it is possible for the couples concerned to be married in a church with two central aisles, seating arrangements for the ceremony will be quite simple but the layout of most churches is not quite so convenient. When there is only one aisle the

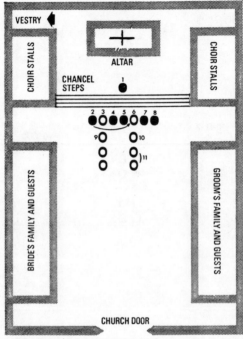

Fig. 7 *The Double Wedding at the chancel steps*

1. Minister
2. Father of both Brides
3. Bride (A)
4. Groom (A)
5. Best Man (A)
6. Bride (B)
7. Groom (B)
8. Best Man (B)
9. Chief Bridesmaid (A)
10. Chief Bridesmaid (B)
11. Attendants

families of the two grooms will have to share the favoured positions at the front of the church on the right, and there may only be a need for one set of ushers.

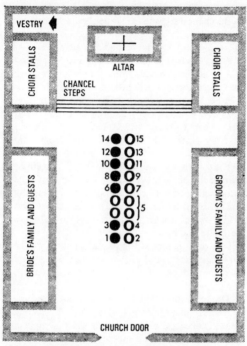

Fig. 8 *The Recession at the Double Wedding*

1. Groom (A)
2. Bride (A)
3. Groom (B)
4. Bride (B)
5. Attendants
6. Brides' Father
7. Mother of Groom (A)
8. Father of Groom (A)
9. Brides' Mother
10. Groom (B) Father
11. Groom (B) Mother
12. Best Man (A)
13. Chief Bridesmaid (A)
14. Best Man (B)
15. Chief Bridesmaid (B)

At the start of the ceremony the two grooms, each with his own best man, will take their places at the head of the aisle, the future husband of the first and eldest bride will stand slightly to the right of the chancel steps to allow the choir and minister to walk past and second groom and his best man will stand on the right of the first pair.

When the brides make their entrance, the eldest will be escorted by her father, the younger bride may be escorted by a brother or another male member of her family. When the procession reaches the chacel steps the first bride will stand next to her groom, on his left; the second bride will take her place to the right of the first couple and her escort can immediately return to his seat.

The ceremony is usually divided into sections with each couple making their vows in turn. The father can give both brides away before returning to his seat. If the brides are not sisters, the second bride's father will stand between the first couple's best man and his own daughter.

It is most common for the brides to share the same attendants, although each should have her own chief bridesmaid to take the flowers while the ceremony is in progress.

The recession is led by the eldest bride and her husband, followed immediately by the second couple. Since the bride's parents can only appear once in the procession the parents of the second groom may have to walk down the aisle together, or escort and be escorted by one chief bridesmaid and one best man.

The Roman Catholic Wedding

According to the law of the land the religious ceremony in the Roman Catholic Church must be accompanied by a civil declaration to legalize the marriage. In the established Church most ministers are authorized to perform the registration of the marriage, but in the Roman Catholic Church registration should be carried out by a state official.

There are two types of Roman Catholic wedding: a simple ceremony and a full Nuptial Mass. The church calendar forbids a Nuptial Mass to take place during Lent and between the first Sunday of Advent and December 26th. A Nuptial Mass cannot be celebrated unless both the bride and groom are Catholics.

The procession, church seating and the exchange of vows at the Catholic wedding are very similar to those of the established Church, but in addition to the wedding ring the groom must present gold and silver to his bride.

Following the exchange of vows, the wedding ring ceremony and the blessing the couple, with two witnesses, proceed to the sacristy where the civil declaration is made, and the register signed and witnessed.

This concludes a simple Catholic ceremony, but in the case of a full Nuptial Mass the bridal party returns once more to the church. The couple take their place behind the sanctuary rails and the best man, parents and attendants take their seats at the front of the church. It is sometimes possible for small stools to be placed at the end of the pews for small attendants to sit on during the Nuptial Mass but if this is not possible the ushers must remember to leave spaces for them when the guests are being directed to their places.

Holy Communion may be taken by any members of the congregation if they so wish.

At the end of the Mass, the recession begins with the bride and groom leading the way and the attendants moving into their places from the pews.

Non Conformist Weddings

These are much more simple in style than those of either the Anglican or Roman Churches, although the wording of the ceremony is almost identical. The best man's duties are the same, however, although if he has never attended a nonconformist wedding he should ask the bride exactly what form the service will take and ask her to explain any minor differences in wording or the order of service.

The Jewish Wedding

When it comes to celebrating the Jewish race can really go to town. Parents often save for years to give their daughter a good send-off and the reception rituals will usually go on long into the night.

It is extremely unlikely that a best man at a Jewish wedding will not himself be a member of the faith, but, if you should find yourself doing the honours, you must inform yourself about all the details of the ceremony, which will differ considerably from those of the Christian Churches.

The wedding ceremony in a synagogue takes place underneath a canopy, which is often beautifully decorated with flowers. The groom is escorted to his place by male members of his family and the same escort will return to the synagogue door to collect the bride and deliver her to her groom's right hand. Without exception the congregation must have their heads covered; the men and women sit on opposite sides of the synagogue.

The details of the ceremony will vary according to the rites of the Orthodox or Reformed Synagogue. The Orthodox service will include the Seven Benedictions, which are chanted by the rabbi, and the groom will break a wine glass beneath his heel to symbolize the destruction of the Temple in Jerusalem.

Although a separate civil contract is made it is still necessary to sign the marriage register at the synagogue and to add the names of two witnesses.

The Civil Wedding

A register office wedding is a simple contract usually made between two people who do not share the same religious beliefs. They may be divorced and unable to remarry in church, or religious convictions may have no meaning for them.

The brief nature of the ceremony does not lend itself to the usual formalities undertaken by the best man at a wedding ceremony. He can hand over the ring to the groom at the appropriate moment in the ceremony, but strictly speaking there is no need for a ring to play any part in the proceedings, although most brides will keep this tradition even if they are willing to dispense with most of the others. The bride and groom will arrive at the register office together, and, in the presence of at least two witnesses, apart from the officiating Registrar, they will declare that there is no lawful impediment to their marriage. They will then call upon the attendant audience to witness their marriage. The register is signed by two witnesses after the bride and groom have signed, and the Registrar and Superintendent Registrar will also add their signatures.

A register office ceremony may take place between sunrise and sunset, which for the purpose of a wedding is always 6 pm even in the summer. It is worth noting that most register offices are closed from noon on a Saturday (usually because the civil officials are out at other people's weddings).

The best man should certainly make himself available to get the couple to the register office on time. Civil weddings run to a strict timetable and if the couple are late they often have to wait until later in the day, or miss their turn altogether.

Normal procedures for a reception can follow the civil wedding, although formal invitations sent out to the guests should request their company at the reception only. Most civil offices are far too small to allow the attendance of more than a dozen close friends and family.

Chapter 9

The Reception

FIRST TO ARRIVE at the reception premises will be the bride and groom, followed by the attendants and parents. You, as best man, should be among the first so that you can speak to the toastmaster about the sequence of events and provide the names of the the speakers. Ask the two sets of parents for any telegrams which arrived at their homes before they left for the wedding and ask the receptionist for any that may have arrived at the hotel.

However efficiently the wedding presents have been dealt with, there will still be a number of people who will turn up at the wedding with carefully wrapped gardening tools and waste-paper bins, not easily sent by post. Speak to the hotel manager about this and ask if a member of the hotel staff could take them up to the room which has been made available for the bride and groom to change in.

The chief bridesmaid should take charge of the bride's bouquet and put it in a cool place while the reception is in progress.

A formal reception timetable for a wedding starting at 2.30 pm could run like this:

2.30 Wedding ceremony begins;

3.30 Bride, groom, attendants and parents arrive at the reception premises;

3.35 The principal members of the wedding party should line up to receive their guests;

3.40 The first guest is announced;

4.40 The toastmaster requests silence for cutting the cake and the speeches;

5.00 The bride and groom leave the reception room to change;

5.20 The best man collects the groom's car keys and the honeymoon luggage. The bride and groom return to the reception room to spend a few minutes with their guests and then lead the way outside for the departure; the best man brings the car around to the front door;

5.30 Bride and groom leave.

The above sequence of events will apply to a buffet reception, but if a sit-down meal has been arranged the guests will be given an aperitif when they have been received by the bride and groom. When the last guest has taken his drink the toastmaster will call for attention and direct everyone to their appointed seats. The cake-cutting ceremony takes place after the final course, but before coffee is served. The bride and groom are often given coffee and cake in their room.

The Receiving Line

There can never be hard and fast rules about this because the situation will vary from wedding to wedding. In most cases where the entrance hall of the hotel permits a large number of people to stand around and wait until they are announced by the toastmaster, and providing that there are no more than a hundred guests, the receiving line will be as follows:

Fig. 9 *The Receiving Line*

1. Best Man (if Toastmaster is not available)
2. Bride's Mother
3. Bride's Father
4. Groom's Mother
5. Groom's Father
6. Bride
7. Groom

A full receiving line will include the bridesmaids and best man, but this is usually a waste of time. When there is a large number of guests the bride and groom have been known to receive on their own. If a toastmaster is not provided, the best man is often called upon to announce the guests.

At this point it should be mentioned that it is absolutely vital for the best man to memorize the names of at least the people most concerned with the wedding whom he will be talking to and about at the reception, however bewildering he may find the sea of faces. If the best man is not good at remembering names it is a good idea to write down and memorize before the reception the names of the following members of the wedding:

1 Bride's mother, father and other close relations;
2 Groom's mother, father and other close relations;
3 The minister;
4 Bridesmaids, pages or other attendants.

Fig. 10 *Top Table Seating*

1. Bride	6. Groom
2. Bride's Father	7. Bride's Mother
3. Groom's Mother	8. Groom's Father
4. Minister	9. Minister's Wife
5. Chief Bridesmaid	10. Best Man

The Wedding Breakfast

This does not mean that the meal must take place in the morning – it is simply the term used for a sit-down meal.

Top table seating will vary according to the

Fig. 11 *Top table seating in special circumstances*

1. Bride
2. Bride's Father*
3. Groom's Mother
4. Best Man
5. Bride's Stepmother
6. Groom
7. Bride's Mother
8. Groom's Father
9. Chief Bridesmaid
10. Bride's Stepfather*

*Whoever is proposing the first toast should sit next to the Bride.

circumstances, but the minister and his wife should be given a place on the top table if they are present at the reception and grace should be said before the meal. One accepted format is shown above.

When a divorce has occurred in a family, the seating arrangements will depend on how amicable everyone concerned is prepared to be for this occasion. The greatest bone of contention arises when the bride's parents have been divorced and the bride has been brought up by her mother and possibly a stepfather. If the bride's own father has remarried and for the purposes of the wedding has asked if he may give his daughter away at the wedding ceremony, he should be given a place at the top table together with his wife.

A seating plan could be arranged as in Fig. 11 but all the people concerned must be approached by the bride and their agreement sought.

If the bride's father gave her away at the wedding ceremony, the courtesy of making the first speech could be extended to her stepfather. Remember that the stepfather will probably have played a large and loving part in the bride's life: this is one way of expressing gratitude. If this should be the case, he could take his seat next to the bride at the top table.

Car Decorations

During the course of the wedding reception someone is bound to organize a sabotage party for the groom's car. Unless you can take the precaution of hiding the car two miles down the road, this is an inevitable wedding-day ritual. Hopefully, no one would ever be foolish enough to interfere with the car's machinery, but here is one word of warning to those who own a covertible with a perspex rear window. Shaving creams used to daub the words 'Just Married' on the back window seem to set up a chemical reaction which abrases the surface, and no amount of cleaning can repair the damage. Perhaps you, as the best man, should stick a notice on the back saying 'NO FUNNY BUSINESS WITH THE WINDOW PLEASE!'

Display of Wedding Presents

Fortunately the custom of displaying wedding

presents at the wedding reception seems to be less popular than it was at one time. If you are in a position to offer advice to the bride or her parents about this point out that it could be asking for trouble. Whereas one would never suspect the motives of guests or hotel staff, it is simply impossible to check on everyone else who may be wandering around the hotel. Any light-fingered member of the community has a golden opportunity to see what spoils there are for the taking in the couple's new home and any professional criminal will have no difficulty in finding out their address.

The other argument against the display of wedding presents is that some people who could only afford a bread board might be rather embarrassed to see it nestling against a canteen of solid silver cutlery, particularly if name tags accompany the gifts.

After the bride and groom have had time to circulate among their guests, and any extra photographs have been taken, or, in the case of a sit-down reception the final course has been finished, the toastmaster will call order for the cake-cutting ceremony and the speeches. Wedding cakes have a thick layer of royal icing which is very difficult to cut neatly, so an incision is often made by the hotel staff before the reception gets under way. As soon as the cake has been cut by the bride and groom, it is whipped away by the catering staff to be cut up for the guests to eat with their coffee. The toastmaster will then announce the speeches:

'Ladies and gentlemen, pray silence for the bride's father' (or close friend of the family).

The bride's father, first in to bat, will thank

everyone for coming to the wedding and say a few words of welcome to his new son-in-law. He concludes by proposing a toast to the bride and groom.

The groom will reply on behalf of his new bride and himself, thanking the first speaker for the toast, the guests for coming to the wedding and for their presents. He may thank the best man for all his good deeds and present him with a small gift as a token of thanks. He concludes his speech by proposing a toast to the bridesmaids. The best man will reply on behalf of the bridesmaids. He will congratulate the groom on his good luck and proceed to read the telegrams (which he must check beforehand to weed out any dubious ones).

After these formalities the bride and groom will retire to their room to change into their going-away clothes.

The best man will collect the groom's car keys and luggage and drive the car around to the front door. He should hand over any documents which he has been keeping for the groom, plus the telegrams which can be read once again at the couple's leisure.

The bride and groom will return to the reception room to spend a few moments with their guests and the chief bridesmaid should return the bouquet to the bride.

Led by the bride and groom the guests and families will congregate outside the hotel. A last round of goodbyes and congratulations, then the bride will throw her bouquet to the next matrimonial victim and the couple will drive away in a flurry of confetti!

Tying up the Loose Ends

The guests will slowly begin to disperse, and if there is another function at the hotel to fcllow the reception, the hotel staff will welcome your help in moving lingering guests out of the reception rooms. Together with the chief bridesmaid you should go up to the changing room and collect the couple's wedding clothes and wedding presents, leaving the room reasonably tidy. Ask the bride's parents if they need help to transport the presents. If there has been a sit-down reception, collect some napkins, place cards and other mementoes, which the bride may like to keep on her return from the honeymoon.

The rest of the wedding cake should be collected from the kitchen staff, to be sent around to people who could not attend the wedding. The top tier of the cake can be used for a future christening, since wedding cakes will keep fresh for years in an air-tight container. Thank the hotel staff for their help, on behalf of the bride and groom, and take the couple's belongings around to the home of the bride's parents. Remember that if the groom hired a morning suit it must be returned as soon as possible.

You could suggest that the bridesmaid visits the couple's new home before they return from their honeymoon, to leave vases of flowers. A small thought like this makes a wonderful homecoming.

Finally, treat yourself and the chief bridesmaid to a stiff drink – you both deserve it!

Chapter 10

Other Receptions

THE RECEPTION discussed in the preceding chapter dealt with an average formal reception where the hotel catering staff undertake all the catering arrangements. There exists a much more formal celebration which includes a dance in the evening, and, at the other end of the scale, there is a simple gathering of friends, with a small buffet, usually held at the home of the bride's parents.

The Dance
A wedding reception which includes a dance will usually start with a wedding celebration held as late in the afternoon as possible. Guests will often arrive at the wedding dressed in their dinner jackets and long dresses, with the exception of the main members of the wedding who will wear formal morning clothes. The latter should be offered facilities to change into dinner clothes after the guests have been received at the reception.

After the wedding the guests will move off to the reception premises, where a cocktail party is held and the guests are formally received. A large buffet or sit-down meal follows the cocktails. The speeches, toasts and the cake-cutting ceremony follow the same sequence as at an afternoon wedding.

When the formalities are over the tables are pushed back and the toastmaster will announce that 'dancing will commence'. The bride and groom lead the dance followed by the chief bridesmaid and the best man, members of the two families and finally the guests. The best man's duties are the same as at any other reception but he must of course be one of the first to ask the bride to dance.

A Simple Reception

This usually, but not always follows a Register Office wedding. If the couple are to be married on a Saturday the wedding must take place in the morning. Facilities for large numbers at a civil wedding are rare and guests invited to such a ceremony will include families and close friends only.

The wedding is followed by an informal lunch at a restaurant and the guests will disperse to prepare for a larger reception held in the evening, perhaps at a hotel, but more often at the home of the bride's parents.

Many catering firms are prepared to come to a private house and provide both the food and all the necessary equipment, but if the catering is to be carried out by the bride's family the best man's duties before this type of reception may be far more complicated.

He will probably be expected to help with the collection of various pieces of equipment: glasses from a nearby pub, sausage rolls and other delicacies from a local bakery. He will probably be put in charge of the drinks for the evening, which could involve a trip round to the off-licence if stocks run low. He may be asked to organize the musical entertainments for the evening, which might mean trips to friends' houses to beg tapes, records and other pieces of musical equipment. In return for all this he may be let off the ordeal of making a wedding speech, but even an informal celebration will require a few words of congratulation. At the end of the evening, having been chief barman, DJ, porter, diplomat and toastmaster, he will probably be required to be chief washer-up!

Chapter 11

The Best Man's Wedding Speech

IF YOU ARE just an ordinary guy with no aspirations to politics or anything else that involves public speaking the idea of having to stand up in front of an audience and entertain them at a wedding will probably colour your thoughts blue for weeks before the big day.

There are three types of speech that the best man can make: the witty speech, the boring speech and the sincere speech.

The art of wit cannot be acquired in a few weeks of practice; nor can anyone be expected to do a good job with someone else's script written specially for the occasion. Remember you are not a television comedian. A professional comedian's success lies in the ability to act, in facial expression and in the confidence that comes with assured popularity. Few ordinary people possess this talent. If you are among the lucky ones who do you will be well aware of your ability and will need little, if any, guidance.

The boring speech comes as a result of **trying**

to prepare a cleverly contrived oration. To a captive audience this is precisely how such a speech will sound; contrived, often flat and in many cases far too long.

The sincere speech is what people want to hear at a wedding. It is unlikely to fail because it explains exactly how you feel and no one should object to this providing you do not go on too long.

Points to remember when making a speech:

1. Speak clearly but not so loudly that you could shatter a pane of glass at ten paces and not as though someone is standing on your windpipe;

2. Never clink the loose change in your pocket;

3. Never shuffle your feet as though you are practising the cha-cha;

4. Never ease your tie away from your collar – you are not on trial for your life;

5. Do not mop your face with a handkerchief – you are not about to pass out;

6. Remember that the audience is not critical – they are there to enjoy themselves; to eat, talk, and congratulate the bride and groom;

7. Consider how *you* feel about speeches made at a social function. Do you sit up brimming with interest and expectancy, or do you think 'Oh no – the speeches – I hope they don't go on for too long'? If you are honest your thoughts will tend to the latter and if the speeches are short, concise, sincere and perhaps witty then you are probably agreeably surprised. Doubtless this is how most of your audience will feel about you.

Your speech will be preceded first by that of the bride's father, who will formally thank everyone for coming to the wedding and welcome his new son-in-law to the family. He will conclude by proposing a toast to the bride and groom.

The groom will then reply on behalf of himself and the bride. He will thank the guests for their good wishes and wedding presents. He should thank his father-in-law for both his daughter's hand and for his toast. He will conclude by proposing a toast to the bridesmaids if there are any. If not, he may well propose the health of the bride's parents and his own in thanks for all their help over the years and for such a splendid wedding.

Your speech will follow. Points to be covered:

1 On behalf of the bridesmaids you thank the groom for his toast and you may add suitable comments of your own;

2 You congratulate the groom on his good luck, possibly telling the audience how the couple first met, if this is not a long story;

3 You conclude by reading the telegrams which are suitable for public hearing, remembering that there may be children and maiden aunts present. You could omit a proportion of the simple congratulatory telegrams if there is a large number of these.

A typical best man's speech could run along these lines:

Ladies and gentlemen, on behalf of the bridesmaids, I should like to thank John for his toast, and I must say that I'm really enjoying myself – the opportunity of being surrounded by a gathering of pretty women doesn't happen every day. It's a pity we're only allowed one bride in this country – I'd marry them all if I could – and if they'd have me!

A lot has been said about the bride today, and I would like to say some more! She looks absolutely gorgeous and she's a fabulous person too. John's a very lucky guy – he's looking so smug and pleased with himself that he doesn't really need any congratulations. Perhaps some of you don't know how all this started.

Well – John was at a party and he tried to phone me to ask where I'd got to. Instead of me he got a wrong number and Susan was on the other end. He says that she sounded like a pretty girl so he asked her for a date . . . need I say more? – except that I wish it was me who made that phone call – the telephone company has never done me such a good turn.

John may not think he needs any congratulations, but I'm going to wish them both all the luck in the world anyway, and I'm sure everyone will agree that this has been a great wedding.

Now, I have to read some of the telegrams:

'Hoping you two never get your wires
crossed again'

Love Tom and Jenny

'Best wishes for the future'

Love from Penny and Chris

etc. etc.

I think that's probably enough for now – if I read them all we'll still be here next week and these two have a plane to catch. Once again John and Susan – all the very best and a long and happy life to you.

However tempted you may be, never mention all the hundreds of girl friends who have figured in the groom's life and if you are best man at a wedding following a previous divorce, or if either of the couple is widowed, do not make any references to the past marriage. And certainly never say anything like 'Better luck this time' – you are supposed to be tactful, remember!

Check List

Names to Remember
    Bride's Mother's Name. Father's Name
    Groom's Mother's Name. Father's Name
    The Minister
    Bridesmaids
    Ushers
    Groom's close relations
    Bride's close relations
    Others?

Leave Home: am/pm
    Collect Buttonholes
    Arrive at Groom's Home: – am/pm

Before leaving, check we have:
    The Ring. Buttonholes. Service Sheets.
    Taxi 'Phone Numbers. Money – Foreign
    Currency.
    Honeymoon Baggage. Travelling Clothes/
        Shoes.
    Telegrams. Umbrellas. Driving Licence/
        Insurance.
    Travel Tickets. Banns Certificate.
    Passports. Innoculation Certificates.

Arrive at Reception Premises: am/pm
   Leave - Honeymoon case
               Travelling Clothes
               Telegrams
               The Groom's car if needed for departure.

Arrive at Church: am/pm
   Hand over Service Sheets to Ushers
   Pay Service Fees
   Photograph of self and Groom'
   Take our places for the Service by - am/pm

The Service Starts: am/pm

After the Service
   Check that Transportation has arrived
   Self available for group photographs
   Leave Taxi 'Phone Numbers with Chief Usher

Leave for Reception about: am/pm
   Give Toastmaster a list of Speakers:
    1 Bride's Father/Close Family Friend:
       Mr. ....
    2 The Groom: Mr.....................................
    3 Self: Mr. ....
   Ask him to announce the speeches at - am/pm

My Speech must, at least, include
    1 Thanks from the Bridesmaids for the Groom's Toast
    2 Congratulate the Groom on his good luck in marrying such a wonderful girl.
    3 Reference to a great Wedding Reception
    4 A selection of the Telegrams.
The Bride and Groom should change at   am/pm
Their transport should be available am/pm
I must recheck his tickets, documents, etc.
They should leave by   am/pm